STRIKE

Sarah Wimbush

Stairwell Books //

Published by Stairwell Books
161 Lowther Street
York, YO31 7LZ

www.stairwellbooks.co.uk
@stairwellbooks

ISBN: 978-1-913432-80-5
p11

Cover photograph © Keith Pattison: Easington 1984.

Sarah Wimbush is a Yorkshire poet and the recipient of a Northern Writers' Award. Her first collection, *Shelling Peas with My Grandmother in the Gorgiolands*, was published with Bloodaxe in 2022. Previous publications include: *The Last Dinosaur in Doncaster* (Smith | Doorstop, 2021) and *Bloodlines* (Seren, 2020). Her poetry has recently appeared in the significant anthologies: *After Sylvia* (Nine Arches Press, 2022) and *Wagtail: The Roma Women's Poetry Anthology* (Butcher's Dog, 2021). A fan of poetry-film, her collaborative piece, *The Pencil Sharpener*, was shortlisted in the 2021 Ó Bhéal Competition. She is a member of York Stanza and Doncaster Read to Write, and a regular at Chemistry Poetry and Spoken Word, Leeds.

Sarah's ancestors were involved in the coal industry across northern England. They worked on the surface as office staff and surveyors, and below ground as hewers, fillers, ostlers, pony-drivers, pumpwrights, sinkers, winders and haulage boys. In 1910, her great-grandfather moved his family from Cossall in Nottinghamshire (the inspiration for Cossethay in D.H. Lawrence's *The Rainbow)* to work at Yorkshire Main – 'a pit they could stand up in'. Her great-great grandfather drowned in an accident at Tinsley Park and her great uncle was killed in a roof fall at Harworth. Her grandad, a ripper, was also crushed in a roof fall at Harworth, learning to walk again at the Miners' Rehabilitation Centre based in the faded grandeur of Firbeck Hall.

For all the men, women, boys and girls, who lived and died in the pursuit of coal, and for the last pits: Abernant; Aberpergwm; Abertillery; Ackton Hall; Agecroft; Allerton Bywater; Annesley; Arkwright; Ashington; Askern; Babbington; Baddesley; Bagworth; Barnburgh; Barony; Barrow; Bates; Bearpark; Bedwas; Bentinck; Bentley; Bersham; Betteshanger; Betws; Bevercotes; Bickershaw; Bilsthorpe; Bilston Glen; Birch Coppice; Blaenant; Blaenserchan; Blidworth; Bold; Bolsover; Brenkley; Brodsworth; Brookhouse; Bullcliffe Wood; Cadeby; Cadley Hill; Calverton; Caphouse/Denby Grange; Celynen North; Celynen South; Clipstone; Comrie; Cortonwood; Cotgrave; Coventry; Creswell; Cronton; Cwm Coedely; Cynheidre; Darfield; Dawdon; Daw Mill; Dearne Valley; Deep Navigation; Dinnington; Dodworth; Donisthorpe; Easington; Ellington; Ellistown; Emley Moor; Eppleton; Ferrymoor Riddings; Florence; Frances; Frickley/South Elmsall; Fryston; Garw/Ffaldau; Gascoigne Wood; Gedling; Glasshoughton; Golborne; Goldthorpe/Highgate; Grimethorpe; Haig; Harworth; Hatfield; Hem Heath/Tretham; Herrington; Hickleton; High Moor; Holditch; Horden; Houghton; Hucknall; Ireland; Kellingley; Killoch; Kinsley; Kiveton Park; Lady Windsor, Abercynon; Lea Hall; Ledston Luck; Linby; Littleton; Longannet Complex; Lynemouth; Maerdy; Maltby; Mansfield; Manton; Manvers; Marine; Markham, Blackwood; Markham, Duckmanton; Markham Main; Measham; Merthyr Vale; Monktonhall; Moorgreen; Murton/Hawthorn; Nantgarw/Windsor; Newstead; North Gawber; North Selby; Nostell; Oakdale; Ollerton; Park Mill; Parkside; Parsonage; Penallta; Penrhiwceiber; Point of Ayr; Polkemmet; Polmaise; Prince of Wales; Pye Hill; Rawdon; Renishaw

Park; Riccall; Rossington; Royston; Rufford; Sacriston; St John's; Savile; Seafield; Seaham; Sharlston; Sherwood; Shirebrook; Shireoaks/Steetley; Silverdale; Silverhill; Silverwood; Six Bells; Snowdown; South Kirkby; South Leicester; Stillingfleet; Sutton; Sutton Manor; Taff Merthyr; Thoresby; Thurcroft; Tilmanstone; Tower; Treeton; Treforgan; Trelewis; Vane Tempest/Seaham; Warsop; Wath; Wearmouth; Welbeck; Westoe; Westthorpe; Wheldale; Whitemoor; Whittle; Whitwell; Whitwick; Wistow; Wolstanton; Woolley; Yorkshire Main.

Markham Main

Afternoons, they meet up
on street corners
like old youths planning revolution.

Gaffers, fathers, brothers –
an hour at the Club with a pint.
Go over the end again, and again.

How they were the last by three days
to stay out in Yorkshire.
How they'd 'gu back tomorra'.

After school, they take the grand-kids
to the Pit Top Playground, look forward
to the night shift at Ikea. Together.

Table of Contents

Our Language

This is the voice. This is the sound of the broad and gubbed; the Undermen, the too-young, the faced-up, the midnight-blue tattooed. These are mouths fit to bust with fault lines and deputy sticks, the crackling of airlocks, motties, cages and tubs; throats riddled with methane and headstocks, gob-stink and dog-ends, of nights and days and afters, and the short walk home as dawn spills over the tip at the end of the houses. This is the language of the pony riders and jumped-up checkweighmen, of Davy lamps and Dudleys, the oncostlads and gaffers, of black-nails and snap-tins, and names like Arthur passed down through time till it's more than a name, it has new meaning like the word GIANT or STONE. It is not dole-wallahs, nor the never-never, nor the light-fingered, nor more to be pitied than talked about, although talked about all the same, it is making your mark with a cross and having faith in what's beneath. It's friendship. It's *fuck the bastards*. This is the tune of haulage boys and shot-firers and Elvis impersonators, their legs smashed to bits at the bottom of shafts and the women who feed everyone's children. Sometimes the words speak for themselves at galas or picket lines, or not at all, on those rare rest days, by a well-stocked lake, where men of rock are silenced by a distant horizon. I could catch this language and write it out for those who want to know, I could place it in their palms to hold like a squab and watch it swell with all its boot rooms and slack, because our language still exists. It roars by gas fires, and at the far table in the Club, and in the living museum beside the image of a man digging forever through a coal seam two foot thick. It is black lung and unwritten songs. It is soup kitchens, work vests, hewers. Picks.

Miners call for non-striking miners to join the strike, Nottinghamshire. 14.04.84. Photographer: © John Sturrock/reportdigital.co.uk

Scargill

i

The dictionary is his Bible. Full stop.

He knows boys who were crushed
with only a handful of adjectives in their tipple tins.

Some words shall always be difficult to pronounce:
Oaks, Huskar, Senghenydd.

ii

He points at the dole-not-coal paddy train,
it will arrive shortly at Platform Do-or-dinosaur.

Rule 41, rules okay, he says
the National Executive Committee says.

Inky corridors begin to infect conservatories.

There could be other words, other skies
but his eyes – blue and infinite – have limitations,
there's one path lads: picket!

iii

Faces crowd into a crown.

Each step up the mountain creaks like a blue back.

He lights the wall of a stadium with his cap lamp,

the stray-dog-kids are coming, he says,
raises his iambic voice, that finger.

4

Arthur Scargill, President of the National Union of Mineworkers 1982 to 2002, speaking at the Barbary Coast Club, Sunderland. 1984. Photographer: © Keith Pattison.

Kick-off

It is always as you stare into the muzzle
of a mountain, the wheel's silence

blasting over-the-top – *giz a knock, pal.*
And the gods, our gods, are played like castles

and kings and rooks – the rank and file
unpicking the scab of no-man's pit-top.

And plod helmets become goalposts.
And a penalty bombs the lines, Keegan

and Beckenbauer, Subbuteo on the hotfoot,
welly boots in the fray. And the orchestra

is a volcano, doubles then quadruples
on the horizon. Boys again, out on the Rec

kicking to win. While in the belly of England
the strike to end all strikes erupts.

Police and pickets play football at Bilsthorpe Colliery, Nottinghamshire. March 1984.
Photographer: © Denis Thorpe. Photograph courtesy of The Guardian.

The NUM

I am here
in your breast pocket,

the size of a bus pass
and the Magna Carta –

been sacked for
been starved for.

My foundations
are federations,

old as the moon
and lassoed to oceans.

You may smash me
between coal imports

and blackcoats
and turncoats,

but I will resolve,
shall gather

in the sediment
to re-emerge as bedrock.

National Union of Mineworkers (NUM) Membership Card. 1985. Photograph courtesy of the National Coal Mining Museum for England.

Coal Imports

Wave after wave
of ships
steam into British waters.

Some say,
there are monsters
down there.

Miners attempt to stop coal imports from Germany and Poland. Wivenhoe Port, Essex. 10.04.84. Photographer: © John Sturrock/reportdigital.co.uk

The Three Feathers

Fear is a creature with wings.
It broods its chad
beneath the downy beat
of a four-chambered heart.

Insular crows.
They raven on the blue thermals
until extinction – that sly old vulture –
splits the atom.

Some flock at dawn
piping their wishbones
across Spencerland
battledore! battledore!

Others drop a doodlebug
through the letterbox.
Words spill into war.
As we choke on the explosion

our red-brick terraces zip together
1926 in the air –
three white plumes
sending us underground.

To THE NUM SECRETARY
ANNESLEY COLLIERY
ANNESLEY
NOTTS

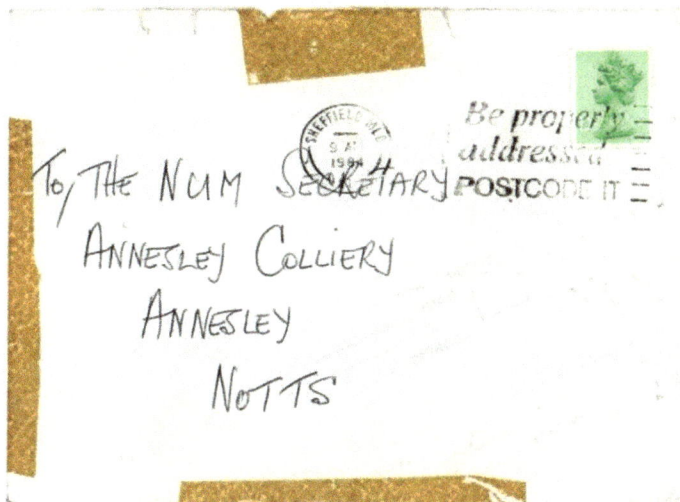

To THE GUTLESS MINERS OF
ANNESLEY
THANK GOD FOR MEN IN
1939

Date-stamped: Sheffield 9th April 1984, predating the NUM NEC meeting on 12th April 1984 and the Special Delegates Conference on 19th April 1984.
Photograph courtesy of © David Amos.

Berry Hill

Brothers, when did this wound
redden between us?
We are not simply *Notts in our blood* –
I'm from Castlecomer, he's from Ukraine.

Don't manride into town pointing
your headboards and ballyrags
like it's Towton – this descent
into Michael Fletcher and the Krays.

Can't you feel the layers
of neo-liberal chaff forming a scab,
now an island? And lads, look, see,
the black picket fence – it's smiling.

Striking miners oppose a working miners' rally, Berry Hill Park, Mansfield, Nottinghamshire. 01.05.84. Photograph: © John Sturrock/reportdigital.co.uk

Queen Coal

These are the women who darn and damn and bide.
They know the exact price of fish, spend their days
as overlockers and home-helps and kallin by the gate,
and nights at Cooplands in nasty green hair nets.
These are the women who understand the thrill
of a worn-out window and the pain of men
smoked to ash, and their mothers were the women
who kept them home to mind the bairns
and serve hungry pantries and donkey-stone doorsteps.
Coal Queens. Pit-brow lasses. Lionesses.
Most can knit. Several have no mice in their cellars
but plenty of rats, girls trapped inside the ring
of a teacup, pallid uncles, dead hearths –
some took a bloody nose, some fought back.
These women are Celts. These women are firecrackers,
born into bones erupting out of the well,
ready for more than a dream of Tom Jones
beside a grin in a glass. What do we think of them
as they raise their linen banners, these monarchs
of Wives' Action Groups and the pit canteen?
What do they sing, these women, as their voice
jemmies the roof, with their Avon and home-perms,
widowhood and thrift – *g'orn lads, g'orn lads!*

First national women's rally in support of striking miners, Barnsley Civic Hall,
Yorkshire. 12.05.84. © NLA/reportdigital.co.uk

This is The BBC

Record. Rewind. Reverse.
We walk through open gates,
a thud of hooves behind us

and so begins the daily spur
three Kingdoms in our face.
Record, rewind, reverse.

Police charge, riot bursts
out down Orgreave's bloody lanes
a thud of hooves behind us –

staffs, shields, dogs, t-shirts,
cameras roll as stones hail.
Record, rewind, reverse.

I'm Spartacus! I'm Spartacus!
Arrest, false charge, detained,
a thud of hooves behind us.

Lies. Lies and more bollocks –
still waiting for Judgement Day.
Record. Rewind. Reverse.
A thud of hooves behind us.

Mounted riot police charge at pickets at Orgreave Coke Works, Sheffield, South Yorkshire. 18.06.84. Photographer: © John Harris/reportdigital.co.uk

Miner running towards a field at Orgreave

Jogging, it seems. He could be catching the last bus
after a night on the lash in Donny town, running
in the slow-mo way some people never seem to rush.
Then again, he could be a boxer on a training regime
along Filey Bay. Or, shirtless and unusually tanned,
having a knock-about with kids on the street. He could be
your dad, or your uncle, or in a few years your old man –
the kind of bloke who can crush a police helmet in his fist
like a walnut or bend a baton with a flick of his thumb.
Small wonder those blue boys put 18-handers
between them and being knocked into kingdom-come.
Mostly, he has that air – you know, not a care,
cigarette in hand as he slaloms live cables and heads
for the wheat fields. Adonis with an Achilles heel.

Mounted riot police chase a striking miner at Orgreave Coke Works, Sheffield, South Yorkshire. 18.06.84. Photographer: © John Harris/reportdigital.co.uk

Mounted policeman canters towards Lesley Boulton

The stave, the stare.
The road, the air,

her bead necklace,
the horse's breath,

her arm, raised,
his arm stretched

pulled up, and flexed,
the lean –

the space between
what was and what

might have been
in white and black –

the hand that grabs her
by the belt

pulls her back.
The woman who lives.

The face that haunts
a thousand pits.

Poster, August 1984. Lesley Boulton at Orgreave, Sheffield, South Yorkshire.
18.06.84. Photographer: © John Harris/reportdigital.co.uk
Poster reads: 'She was only trying to help… LESLEY Boulton lifts up her arm to
protect herself from a police baton, writes *Joy Copley*. Her crime? She was trying
to help a picket with crushed ribs outside Orgreave coking works.'

The Kiss

Not Klimt's golden robes
or the marble passion
of Rodin's hellish embrace.
Not the pop of Lichtenstein
or Man Ray's dreamy rayogram
where touch burns
into light and shade.

No, this is an older buss
from that darker, deeper place
a blue breath
offering the universe
inside a Morabito kiss.
Welcoming him back
who will they be then?

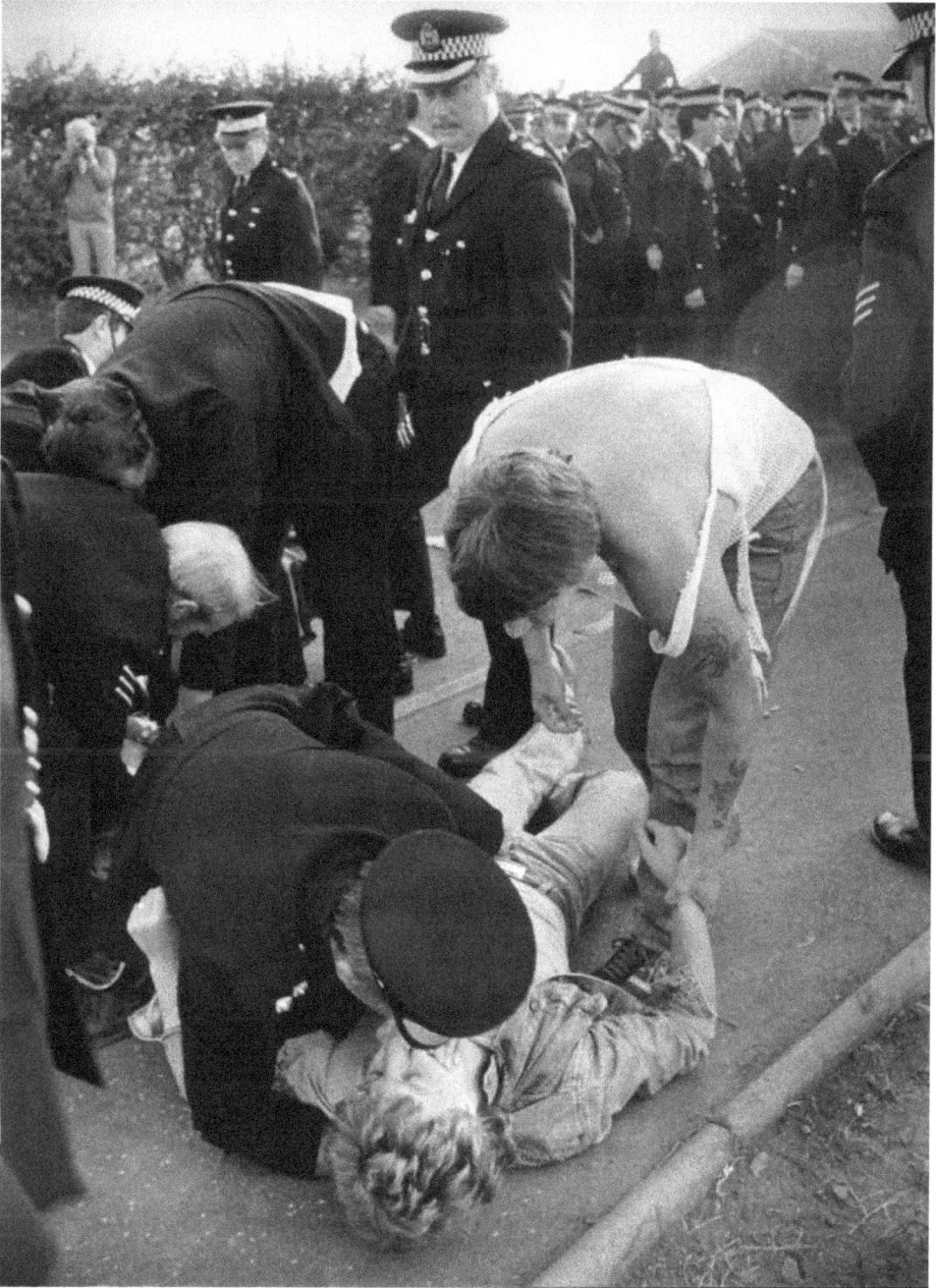

Police inspector gives an injured picket the kiss of life, Bilston Glen Colliery, Scotland.
July 1984. Photographer: © Tom Kidd.

Picture Man

Pockets stuffed with bobbins of *HP5*,
wine gums for dinner and tea, a tripod
slung over his shoulder like a pit shovel.

Five months already, snapping the streets
of Wild West villages being ground into coal dust –
his other eye on the chorus-line police.

The shutter button clicks
and John Harris forever eats carrots,
mash and gravy in Kersley pit canteen.

Later, his blonde locks go to grey
and his back will ping like knicker elastic –
the photographers' bane. But for now

days consist of tip-offs and tones of Orgreave
and Markham Main: a riot shield,
bed-sheet banners, pickets soaked in blood

thrown into the back of a van –
the man who collects monochrome souls
on ribbons of amber

his gaze all pixels and exposure,
his mind a dark chamber of chemical stability,
hands that lift diamonds to his seer's eye.

John Harris, one of several photographers who documented the strike from inside the community. Kersley Colliery kitchen, Coventry, West Midlands. 04.07.84. © John Harris/reportdigital.co.uk

Picketing at Penrhiwceiber

No slack in my hairline,
no crease of grease
across the nape of my neck –
just blue jeans, sunshine

and that scent,
not PHB soap but valley grass,
my daughter's chubby legs
across my thigh

the knee of the hill splayed
beside cogs and cables
iron and steel –
dour and rooted, and still.

Family Day Picket, Penrhiwceiber Colliery, South Wales. 05.07.84.
Photographer: © John Harris/reportdigital.co.uk

Women's Support Groups

They stand on picket lines
with wives from other countries

they stand in Welfare Halls
buying rags not fit for jumble,

they stand at universities
they stand behind a mic,

they stand in police stations,
tube stations, the WI.

They stand outside No.10
they stand out in the snow,

they stand up to the dark forces
and to those who break the code,

they stand beside their husbands
instead of one step behind,

and pull their daughters forward
and stand them in the light.

Rhymney Valley Women Support Group, London during the 'Save Penallta' campaign. 1984. By permission of Amgueddfa Cymru – Museum Wales.

STOP

It starts with hearts. Red and broken
on a soapbox behind a criss-cross
of barbed wire. We pull up a car tyre

drag shop fittings out of a ditch,
throw on sapling oaks, half a besom,
unhinge a litter bin. The village comes out

in support, donates a lion's roar
and a bedstead in case of a nifty kip
and more: an oil drum and a strip-a-gram

for entertainment; skinny roll-ups
and chips and scraps for snap; Welly lock-ins
and two football teams to keep us sane.

Mothers bolster us with hydraulic chocks
and builder's brew – housecoat grenades –
a window cleaner gifts his ladder

for a quick escape. All anchored down
with women's tights and washing line.
And yet, we wonder, how far do powder-monkeys

and rippers need to go to save their jobs?
Still, we stand firm on the wooden plank.
We are stoked, and black and white,

lads and dads; eye to eye, pole to pole
beside the winding gear.
This barricade is our pyramid

our eagle's nest on Everest, our stage.
They beckon from afar *call it time, fellas.*
We show a sign, we have our say.

Miners build a barricade after police get a strikebreaker into Rossington Colliery, Doncaster, South Yorkshire. 09.07.84.
Photographer: © John Harris/reportdigital.co.uk

Our Lady of the Pit Canteen

You may have jacked and packed pit props
on the roadways to hell,
and raised 14,000 tonne week on week
ruled by the bell,
and rode a ghost train through the muck
a fun fair would be proud of
and thanked the Mother Mary
every time the pit cage docked.

You may have scrubbed a fella's shoulders
in the pit-head baths
and dressed up as a bunny girl
at Butlins for the laugh,
and fed the grids and metal steeds
and warmed the hearths of Britain,
and after that blasted knee
drudged as sweeper on pit bottom

and stood by flying pickets
as you watched a pal walk through,
and riddled spoil at twilight
for half a sack of coal
and gone down at 15
and now you're coughing up the black,
but I'll 'ave tha guts fa garters
if them dishes aren't brought back!

Woman and striking miners at the Welfare Canteen, Houghton Main, South Yorkshire. 03.08.84. Photograph: © John Smith/Report IFL Archive/reportdigital.co.uk

Women Against Pit Closures

She blooms,
badged and blue-jeaned
in the sunshine.

In the shadows –
her husband
her father
her sons,

the gate
the hearth
the alarm clock, ringing.

This hybrid rose –
her eyes, anthracite on fire,
her lips, the curve of a pickaxe.

New Aphrodite.
One of the first
to clamber up, up, up
and over
the pit-yard wall.

WAPC Miner's wife from Maltby, South Yorkshire, at a demonstration. 11.08.84.
© NLA/reportdigital.co.uk

Kinnock

i

On his watch, the damp medal of office ticks.

On his watch there is a rusting eye.

He whispers *ballot* into the blindness
of those who wind the gears.

ii

Victorian mine-workings worry a fissure –
the rock face trembling like a hairspring.

Millions of gallons of black blood are about to be spilt.

Facing forwards, he feels the breeze from the crystal forest.
Facing inward, he dreams of a wand.

iii

Some say he is a funeral mute; a man compressed
between left and left.

Some shall say he was father to Blair.

When will you raise a hand to strike the hour?

Arthur Scargill, President of the NUM (left), Neil Kinnock, leader of the Labour Party, and Peter Heathfield (right) at Durham Miners' Gala. 14.07.84.
Photographer: © Stephano Cagnoni/reportdigital.co.uk

Standards

The Miners United shall never be defeated! Solidarity Forever. Butcher MacGregor – MACKS AXE. Turn Orgreave into Saltley. STOP the POLICE STATE. Maggie – OUT! OUT! OUT! Close a Pit, Kill a Village. Coal Not Dole. SAVE OUR PITS. It's not just miners' jobs they're fighting for. NUM – Stop the Split! Dig Deep for the Miners. Unity is Strength. WE WON'T FORGET THE SCABS. Jobs Not Jail. Hands off our Union. My Dad's a Striking Miner. Maggie's Boot Boys. They Shall Not Starve. NO SURRENDER. Coal, the Nation's Energy Future. Wanted: A job, that's all we ask. Go home Yank. I Never Scabbed. CLASS AGAINST CLASS. If the Tories get up your nose: Picket. Stop Pit Closures. Your fight is our fight. Women Against Pit Closures. Women Support the Miners. Miners' Wives Action Group. Miners' Family Support Group. He Works While You Strike. Act your age M'Gregor, DIE NOW. Join the breadline, help keep the miners supplied. Keep Pits Open. Give Youth a Future. Which Side Are You On? Pits and Perverts. STOP: Official NUM Picket. All Out! Turn sympathy into action. Go in and hit them hard. V I C T I M I S A T I O N! No pit is safe! BBC, Tell The Truth!! Victory to the Miners...

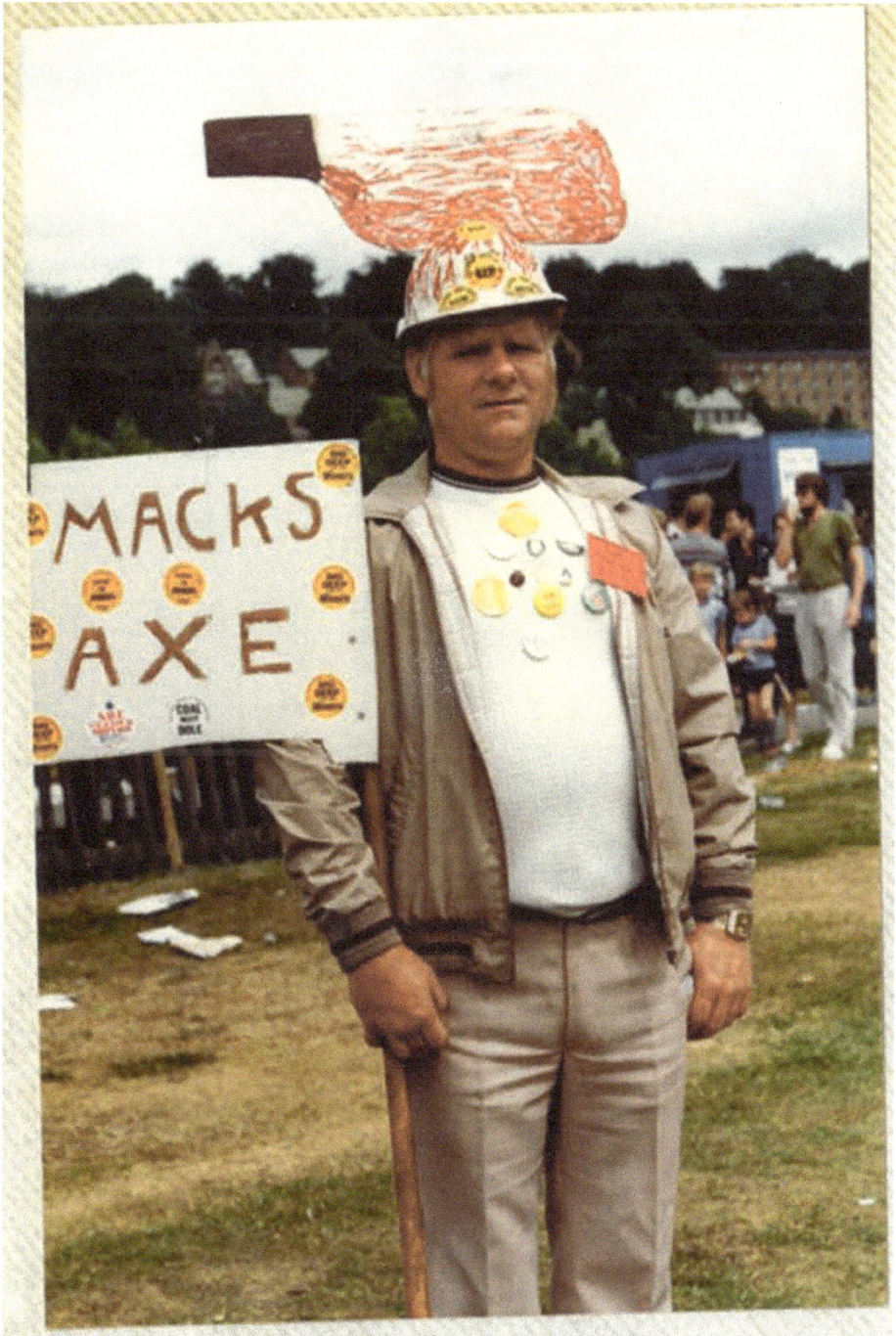

Miner at a rally, 1984. Photograph courtesy of the National Coal Mining Museum for England.

Thatcher

Her Majesty
of backcomb and pearls.
Blonde bombshell, iron-handbagged
and twice the man.

No milk monitor here; eyes sapphire
and Caligula,
hoarder of bituminous and DSS payments.

Who is the mob?
Who are the enemy within?

Pit villages Prometheus Bound
by Back-to-Work incentives: redundancy bribery,
sell-your-soul Christmas bonus –

her puppeteering,
her bloody woman's hands.

Gwent Food Fund poster 1984-85. With images of Margaret Thatcher and Ian MacGregor. By permission of Amgueddfa Cymru – Museum Wales.

Silver Birch

He is Maggie's Judas.
David Hart's bankrolled doofus.

An Ephialtes hole in the crowd,
a blacklegging cow-towing yowl.

He is a rimmer of the night.
He is a sinner in the fight.

A pebble in the pond; gale
and gorged on fame and coal dust.

There can be no pardon.
There shall be no forgiveness

for this Faustian whitedamp Dorian Gray –
no one with a nobody face.

Chris Butcher, Bevercotes' working miner. New Ollerton, Nottinghamshire. 06.08.84.
Photographer: © Peter Arkell/reportdigital.co.uk

'BASTARD NACODS SCABS'

National Association of Colliery Overmen, Deputies & Shotfirers

The pal who leaves a bus ticket
on the collection plate

says he'll see his kids Friday
then dumps them for a date,

roars like a lion
but acts like a mouse,

bald as a brick
and part of the house.

Powder magazine at Lady Windsor/Abercynon Colliery 1984-85. By permission of Amgueddfa Cymru – Museum Wales. Photographer: © Ceri Thompson.

Miner Falling Backwards

I have pin-balled through roadblocks.
I have been driven into the 6 o'clock push,
the dark police waving my Queen's face
in my face. These are my stones.
      This road is my street.

I am your coal-man with clean hands,
brother to *The Dirty Thirty* and our old muckers
at the Alamo, while *I'malrightJack* men
(dead-men walking) are coached-in
      with armies of provocateurs.

Spun from Working-class-Hero to Enigma 23,
I stand before you in my jumble jumper,
tab end in my wallet, Eris hanging me
by a crime with her number on it
      – nothing to hold onto.

Picket is arrested and photographed by police at Hunterston, Scotland, where coal and iron ore are being shipped in for Ravenscraig Steelworks. 06.10.84
© NLA/reportdigital.co.uk

Miners Leaning Forwards

Mortal. Men cropped and cast
into grey corners.

Men as sticks, men as shadow.

Men's pockets lined with bits of string.
Seams. Grit.

Men of rank bound to serve
King Tut and Lord Cardigan.

They gather around hardship money
like new fathers.

Men receive hardship money at Easington Colliery, County Durham. 1984.
Photographer: © Keith Pattison.

Coal Men at Cwmcynon Tip, Penrhiwceiber

Back to backs
swoop across the colosseum.
An army waits by chill windows
as three kings march
over bombarded slack.

Men of Atlas, their world:
a sieve-shield, a trident,
Santa sacks loaded
with black diamonds.
Uphill, all the way back
to those whistling chimneys.

Riddling coal at the old Cwmcynon Tip (colliery closed in 1949), Penrhiwceiber, Wales. By Permission of Rhondda Cynon Taf Libraries.

The Police, The Miners' Wives, Their Children

Easington
blanks
Southern occupation –

perspex wings
flexing
behind Adrian's wall.

Action Man
takes the measure
of the enemy,

or perhaps
he's back home
pegging out nappies

wondering,
what has he been
reduced to.

Joanne, Gillian and Kate Handy with Brenda Robinson overlooked by riot police on the back of Cuba Street looking towards pit yard railway siding, Easington, County Durham. 1984. Photographer: © Keith Pattison.

Strikebreaker

i

The path is blackness and never ending.
The path is my slip and I vote with my feet.

There is light in the distance but what kind of light?
Here, there is nothing but snouts, cow's udder,
chittlins, and for pence, the heart of a beast.

I am light in the darkness but what kind of beam.
The path is my slip and I vote with my feet.

ii

My heart is alive again, pulsing with gozzers,
I am black in the daylight, but what shade of black?

I swap each day's catch for a tin of corned beef,
feed my father, my kids. At the end of the season
I land serpent, lower the cutlass back into the deep.

The black is my path and never mending.
The path is my slip and I vote with my feet.

Police escort a working miner home from Easington Colliery, County Durham. 1984.
Photographer: © Keith Pattison.

People who support the Miners

People nailed to a lathe.
People who grow onions.
People from Borehamwood and Rottingdean.
People from Welsh National Opera
playing Mozart's flute quartet in a shopping centre.
Bus drivers and people who own Rottweilers.
People who greet you with *bonjour, privyet, g'day*.
People in vardos and people in tiaras.
People donating potatoes to soup kitchens
by the tonne every Tuesday.
Dockers, rockers and people on overtime.
People who are tagged.
People with gas fires.
Policemen.
Bevin Boys.
Greenham women.
The unemployed.
People who photograph people being battered
with truncheons.
Football clubs, bridge clubs, the funny handshake club.
Queer people, beer people, God people,
the Afro-Caribbean Centre, Springsteen,
The Sikh Society... Father Christmas.
People who are children of the people who lived
and died on the blunt end of a pick.

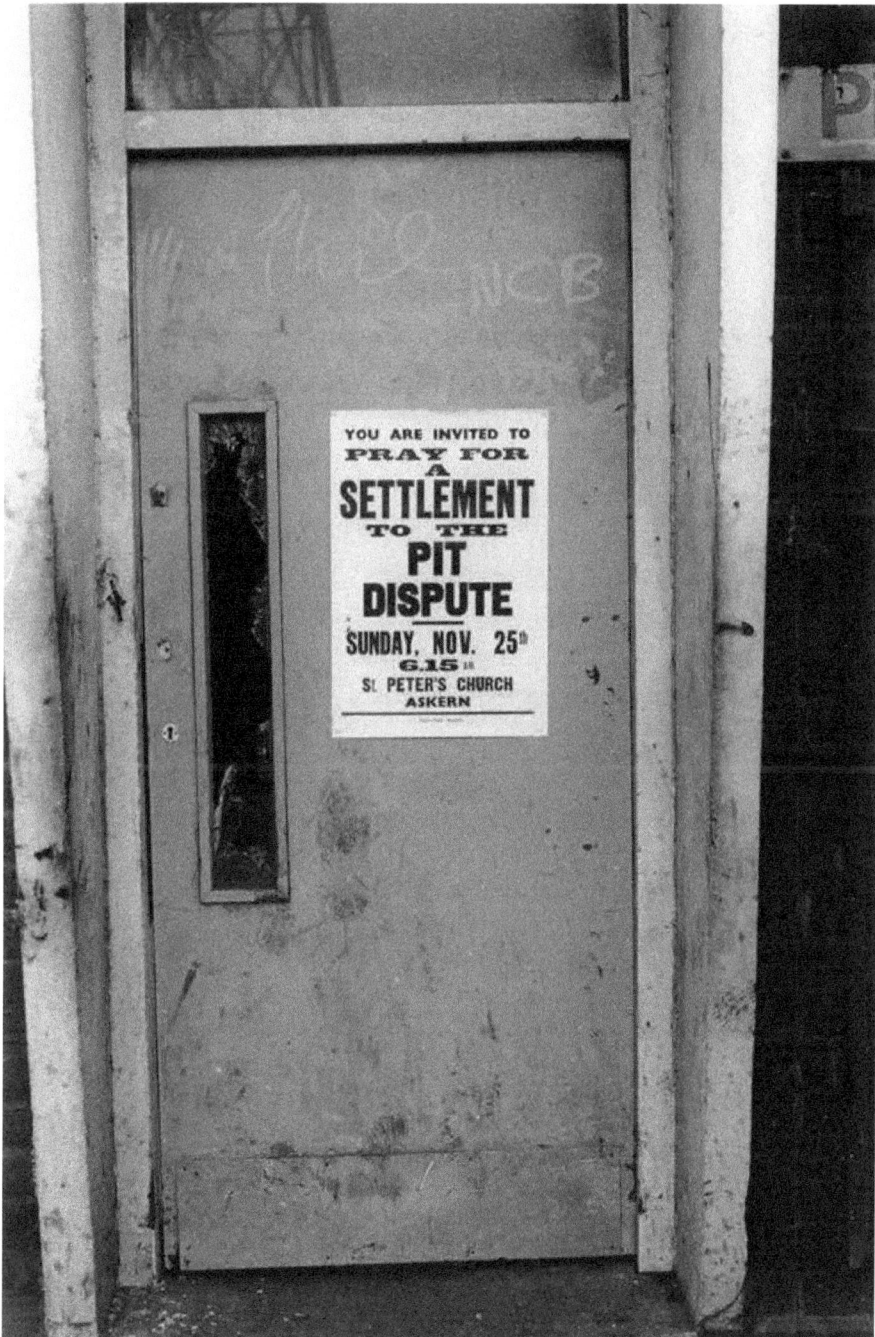

Church poster. Askern Colliery, Doncaster, South Yorkshire. November 1984.
Photographer: © Ken Wilkinson, image courtesy of the National Coal Mining
Museum for England.

Pits and Perverts

Come, dance around our banners
lift the blindfolds from your eyes,
top-up buckets with the readies and *Respect*,
tell me why, oh, tell me why.

Come dance with the Great Atlantic Fault
these coal-cutters, these dark hearts,
Relax among rainbows and small town boys –
with us, they shall not starve.

There are rocks in our closets,
Love and Pride in our snap tins,
from Gay's The Word bookshop to Dulais Valley Lodge
to semis in Milton Keynes.

We are the red-lipped and 'Martha Scargill'
we are the spirit of Turing and Wilde,
we are gay, straight and the undecided,
kids of the coalface and those in denial.

Spin me right 'round, baby
queens and kings of the underground,
hand in hand across the divide –
no surrender, forever proud.

Photograph of an original 'Pits and Perverts' benefit concert poster designed by artist Kevin Franklin. December 1984. By permission of Amgueddfa Cymru – Museum Wales and © Kevin Franklin.

Boy Riddlers

No wooden sled or carrot for a nose
only soggy jeans in a frozen maw.
Junior excavators, waist deep
in the whiteout on Cwmcynon tip,
flattened after Aberfan.
Snood-face and lads-lost numb
in Woolworth anoraks; spade-boy,
hoar-eyed and black-blushered
digging for Penrhiwceiber.
Spoil riddled through a shopping basket,
then topping-up the spud sack
with alchemies of silvered bituminous.
300 million years of compression
dripping through their hands.

Boys riddling coal at the old Cwmcynon Tip (colliery closed in 1949), Penrhiwceiber, Wales. By Permission of Rhondda Cynon Taf Libraries.

The Black Hole

When this Welfare Hall
is full with empty spaces

when there is only the stroke
of a muffled drum,

we will bear our white eyes
and grey faces –

the ground rushing to meet us,
windows blown apart by the sun.

Voting to end the strike with no agreement. Easington Miners' Welfare Hall, County Durham. February 1985. Photographer: © Keith Pattison.

The Enemy

after The Ridley Plan

Enemy behind a riot shield
Enemy by the gate
Enemy driving a coal truck
Enemy on a plate
Enemy twisting the DSS
Enemy printing bull
Enemy burning photographs
Enemy pays the Enemies' bills

Enemy waving tenners
Enemy raking it in
Enemy living next door
Enemy as kin
Enemy ditch their epaulettes
Enemy waits for dawn
Enemy cries *casus belli*
Enemy bends every law

Enemy sacking the black hills
Enemy caps the coal –
fills the shaft
snaps the drill
breaks the cage
douse the lamp
grass the stacks...
a wheel mute in a ditch
a worm swallowing its own tail.

Askern Colliery, Doncaster, South Yorkshire. 1984-85. Photographer: © Ken Wilkinson, image courtesy of the National Coal Mining Museum for England.

The Flat Cap

40 years wrapped in an Evening Post sports page
at the back of the wardrobe or the bits-and-bobs drawer,

Coal Not Dole badges flogged for loose change on Ebay –
the cap itself charity-shopped, or if they can't be arsed

binned then dumped in landfill. In time,
archaeologists from the Rare Civilisations Department

might unearth the object (with a virtual toothbrush) –
petrified, but still intact. Experts debate the cap's origins

why the pin-holes – what about the Yorkshire rain?
The Lead Curator's theory, an inauguration head-dress

threaded with campion and worn by a king. Peoples
dock at the Intergalactic Museum keen to see

this strange discovery and our descendants might wonder,
what kind of man would have worn such a thing?

Striking miner, Brookhouse Pit, Sheffield, South Yorkshire. 28.02.85.
Photographer: © John Harris/reportdigital.co.uk

Backhaul

We are voyagers without oar or map –
Titans, Light Brigaders, double-shifts.
We are headscarves tucked inside anoraks.
We are matinee jackets and hieroglyphs.

Look, how we search for the sun.
Look how we sail in a less travelled craft.
New framework knitters, our brothers undone,
we that have lived in the magician's hat.

A camera in the crowd nets the hour,
great black-backed gulls now caged and clipped
the main sail is appliqued with honour,
the heapstead a reef and we are the ship.

Our people are bound by Jack Tar masters.
Our babies sit up in their prams looking back.
We go down on Hobson's hook, line and anchor
our colours raised, our dove brass.

One day, and soon, you too shall feel the fell,
will ask: how did it ever come to this?
We that would do it all again.
We that gave and gave. And give.

The strike ends on 3rd March 1985. The Women's Support Group leads the return to work at Rossington Colliery, Doncaster, South Yorkshire. 04.03.85.
Photographer: © John Harris/reportdigital.co.uk

Closure

Boulders ebb to shingle
on the pithead.
Washed ashore,
they will blister
and dissolve
into a kingdom
of white dwarfs.
A dusty old gull flaps
above the closed shop
as if to say, *I told you so,*
and the earth
will meet itself again
and seams shall fall
back to sleep.
And the cutters' chatter
is retold as a pickaxe,
and happy misery lives
in a can of Special Brew.
And the city commissions
an art installation
out of steel-toe caps
and Davy lamps.
And we will watch
their manhoods
dangle before us
on meat hooks –
a marble stare
on each coal face.

Rose Heyworth Colliery (Abertillery New Mine, Wales). The manager, Mr Williams, announces closure to the afternoon shift as they wait to go down. The pit closes on 9th October 1985. By permission of Amgueddfa Cymru – Museum Wales.

Victimisation

In that moment a pebble became a planet
and he was the one that bowled it.

Within the hour he got spotted
rocking a scab bus over at Polkemmet

while simultaneously giving the finger
at Betteshanger and Whitwick.

And for certain, months later he was still
up to no good. With Lord Lucan in the crowd

he buried a Welsh bobby's helmet
smack bang in the centre of Creswell gates.

By Christmas he'd made the front page –
Man in a Donkey Jacket and Bank-robber Tights

Chain-saws Lee Hall's Coal Board Signage –
yes, it was definitely him. He stoved in

any number of strikebreakers' windows,
and on 3rd March '85, after a life drowning

in coal dust, the Coal Board announced:
he had never existed.

Amnesty badge for Victimised Miners, 1986. Actual diameter: 26mm. By permission of Amgueddfa Cymru – Museum Wales.

Coal Kid

Who knitted that jumper?

Do you sleep in it
and what colour are those words?

Who is the good boy walking behind you?

When did the sole begin to come away
on your shoe?

Were you hand-painting earlier or riddling coal?

Is it acceptable to say emaciated in front of a boy?

How many lost boys does it take to eat
a bag of scraps?

Have you ever had a dream?

Will there be extra beans for doing the chippy run?

Did Thatcher pin this picture on her fridge?

Trick question: how many boys died
down Markham Main?

Stones, do your eyes feel like stones?

Does the wool itch like a cloak of dead shrews?

Why can't you look at me, boy?

Children coming back from the chip shop, Armthorpe (Markham Main Colliery), South Yorkshire. Back of jumper reads 'FOR MY DAD'. 1986.
Photographer: © Peter Arkell/reportdigital.co.uk

Ballot Box

Hearse-black. Slapped. Kissed.
The jaws of a baited bear.

Imagine, all that hope
in one   small   dark   place.

Melted down,
they will be parts for Puntos

buzzing across the horizon.
Amazon cathedrals. Coffin nails.

Colliery Ballot Box. Photograph courtesy of the National Coal Mining Museum for England.

Death by Strike

in memory of those who died

Strike is a black lily
falling through the air
like a broken house brick.

Strike is the pressure
of a coal wagon
on a picket line at Ferrybridge.

Strike is a caber
tossed onto a Ford Cortina
inside a concrete block.

Strike is a fist beating fast.
Strike is a dreamcatcher
– he'd got branches in his hand.

Strike is a boy scratching at slack.
Entombment.
The weight of snow.

March to commemorate the death of David Jones who died while picketing. 16.03.85.
Photographer: © John Sturrock/reportdigital.co.uk

Notes

Scargill (p4) – On 19th April 1984 the NUM Special Delegates Conference authorised Rule 41, permitting area strikes in the hope of a domino effect of strike action. The necessary 55% majority in a national strike ballot was felt to be unachievable. *'Huskar'* 1838 – 26 children drowned which resulted in the 1842 Mines Act prohibiting girls, and boys under 10, from working underground. *'Oaks'* 1856 – 388 miners and 27 rescuers died. *'Senghenydd'* 1913 – Despite a disaster in 1901 killing 81 miners, and the Coal Mines Act 1911 requiring a ventilation system which was ignored, 439 men and boys and one rescuer died in a series of catastrophic explosions.

Berry Hill (p14) – In an extreme case of intimidation strikebreaker Michael Fletcher was attacked in his home by masked men wielding pickaxe handles while his family hid upstairs.

This is The BBC (p18) – 'The BBC acknowledged some years ago that it made a mistake over the sequence of events at Orgreave… it was a mistake made in the haste of putting the news together. The end result was that the editor inadvertently reversed the occurrence of the actions of the police and the pickets.' – The BBC July 1991. See: *Orgreave Truth and Justice Campaign*.

The Kiss (p24) – 'Morabito kiss' is inspired by Morabito's Pulitzer prize-winning photograph, *Kiss of Life*.

STOP (p32) – 'pole to pole' is a quote from 'Black as the pit from pole to pole' in Invictus by William Ernest Henley.

Standards (p40) – 'Macks Axe' is a reference to Ian MacGregor (Chairman of the National Coal Board, 1983–

1986) also known as 'Mac the Knife' and 'Thatcher's Hatchet Man'.

Thatcher (p42) – French President François Mitterrand described Margaret Thatcher (UK Prime Minister 1979–1990) as having 'the eyes of Caligula, but the mouth of Marilyn Monroe'. Thatcher was also known in Whitehall as TBW – 'that bloody woman'.

Silver Birch (p44) – Chris Butcher, labelled 'Silver Birch' by the media, organised the Nottinghamshire Working Miners' Committee. NWMC was reputedly financed by the Mail on Sunday and David Hart.

'BASTARD NACODS SCABS' (p46) – No miner could work without a Deputy or Overman supervising the shift. Most NACODS members refused to cross NUM picket lines. When NACODS eventually voted to strike in September 1984, their leaders revoked that strike action in exchange for a worthless deal of colliery reviews with the NCB.

Pits and Perverts (p60) – The *Pits and Perverts* benefit concert was organised by Lesbians and Gays Support the Miners, raising £5,650 (£18,000 in 2024). 'Respect' is from *A Little Respect* by Erasure, 1988; 'tell me why' is from *Why* by Bronski Beat, 1984; 'Relax' is by Frankie Goes to Hollywood, 1983; 'small town boys' is from Bronski Beat's *Smalltown Boy*, 1984; 'Love and Pride' is by King, 1984; 'Gay, straight and the undecided' is from the film *Pride*, 2014; 'Spin me right 'round, baby' is from *You Spin Me Round (Like a Record)* by Dead or Alive, 1984.

The Black Hole (p64) – 'muffled drum' is a quote from Funeral Blues by W.H. Auden.

Death by Strike (p80) – David Jones (24) died after being hit by a brick on a picket line at Ollerton; Joe Green (55) was run over by a coal lorry while picketing at Ferrybridge power station; David Wilkie (35) was driving a working miner to Merthyr Vale, when two striking miners pushed a concrete block from a bridge onto his taxi, killing Wilkie; Jimmy Jones and Terry Leaves died on their way to picket duty in South Wales; *'he'd got branches in his hand'* is a quote from The Two Magicians by Paul Bentley; Eric Knaper was fatally injured while picking coal, and in separate incidents Paul Womersley (14), and brothers Paul (15) and Darren Holmes (14) died after being buried beneath collapsing spoil tips.

Acknowledgements

Versions of some of the poems first appeared in *Abridged, Acumen, Alba, Black Nore Review, The Bread and Roses Anthology 2019, Culture Matters, Dream Catcher, The Morning Star, The North, Northern Gravy, Pennine Platform, PN Review, Poetry Salzburg Review, Poetry Wales, Stand.*

'Our Language' and 'Markham Main' were included in The *Last Dinosaur in Doncaster* (Smith | Doorstop, 2021), and later with 'STOP' in my first collection *Shelling Peas with My Grandmother in the Gorgiolands* (Bloodaxe, 2022).

Thank you to Neil Astley at Bloodaxe Books, Ann and Peter Sansom at The Poetry Business, Carole Bromley, John I. Clarke, Phil Connelly, Andy Croft at Smokestack Books, Ralph Dartford, Tracy Dawson, Julia Deakin, Doncaster Read to Write, Danielle Hope, Freya Jackson, Ian McMillan, Ian Parks, Clare Pollard, Wendy Pratt, Seren Books, Amy Wack, Joe Williams and York Stanza for supporting the idea of this book or for comments on some of these poems. Special thanks to Stuart Pickford. Special thanks also to Rose and Alan at Stairwell Books for their production skill and enthusiasm.

Thank you to the National Coal Mining Museum England; Amgueddfa Cymru – Museum Wales and the Big Pit; the National Mining Museum Scotland; Lesbians and Gays Support the Miners; Northern Mine Research Society; reportdigital; Rhondda Cynon Taf Libraries and The Guardian for giving me access to these incredible images, or for being invaluable sources of information, or both. Particular thanks to David Amos, Peter Arkell, David Bell, Stephano Cagnoni, Kevin Franklin, Joe Guinan, John Harris, Rebecca Hudson, Menna James, Kay Kays, Tom Kidd, John Smith, John Sturrock, Ceri Thompson,

Denis Thorpe, Ken Wilkinson. A huge thank you to Keith Pattison.

The Flat Cap was made into a poetry-film in collaboration with FEP and can be viewed on youtube.com/video/tOppkZbAPQg

I am grateful to the Society of Authors for the Authors' Foundation Grant which enabled me to complete this collection.

Other anthologies and collections available from Stairwell Books

For further information please contact rose@stairwellbooks.com

www.stairwellbooks.co.uk
@stairwellbooks

Milton Keynes UK
Ingram Content Group UK Ltd.
UKHW051037170124
436172UK00004B/15

9 781913 432805